100 Proof Isn't for the Fainthearted

Vanessa C. Streng

100 Proof Isn't for the Fainthearted is my first personal collection of poetry. This piece exposes the emotions from the deepest parts within us in order to face our pain and heartbreak head on. I think we are all a little sad in our own way, and I believe the only way to heal is to feel everything all over again. This collection allows readers to connect with all the locked-up feelings hiding in the corners of our brokenness. We all deserve some healing. And some happy.

5 months later he finally asked,
how could I ever make it up to you? To erase the pain. The hurt. And the heartbreak.
100 proof pouring down my throat I set the bottle down and said,
Treat the next one right.

Table of Contents

the chaos

She whispered softly to me, *write something that will leave me speechless, but will bring me to a thousand questions.* As I gazed into her deep blue eyes my pen caressed the page as truth poured out of me. You are a million words and phrases that can be tied together to make beautiful similes of love and passion when written on a blank page but sadly I am no poet and there are no more pages.

-sequel

How do I explain to the woman who carried me within her as the world tried to pull her down from her shoulders every step of the way, that I find it hard to walk alone.

-mama

I want you to be so happy that flowers grow from your eyes and your tears only water them, but I am weeds. I will take your roses, tulips and sunflowers and I will make them my enemies. I will rip every single one from your soul, your roots shriveled and broken in half, do not place me in your garden. Do not have me in your life.

-not all is good

The world deems it unacceptable to talk
about sex yet acceptable to talk about love.
As if it is more common. More understood.
We paint them to be different entities so
when she spreads her legs, we teach young
girls that boys can spell love with their
tongues.

-choices

"I hope you're happy now"
Is the saddest sound of them all.
As if you couldn't make them happy to begin with,
And you do not know what their happiness looks like.
It means you gave them your happy, and instead it made you sad.
And lonely.
And you secretly hope
They are too.

-blinded

Yelling at her for all the things she does
wrong may be a way to fix her problems
until she does them all the time- just to get
your attention. She craves any form of
emotion from you. She mixes up anger with
passion and
she calls this love.
Misery and loneliness have no place
here. This is called abandonment.

-neglect

The devil does not look like the devil. He looks like an angel. I'm sure you've met him.

-fool me twice

How do I tell my father, the only man
that's ever truly loved me, that he's the
only man
that's ever truly loved me.

-you can't

Insomniacs are guilty of living with little
monsters who love to conjure up
nightmares in the dark
because sadness never sleeps.

-up all day

We seek closure because books may have endings, but they do not close themselves.

-I've tried

Look at all the rocks that have been
thrown at you and
how you've used them to build a castle.

-conquer

Sadness hangs over us like the small powerless wings of a baby bird, convinced the only way out of her cage is to jump.

-leap of faith

We hold the power to love, not to be loved. We find hate in not being loved, so we begin to search for love in hate and call it love.

-neatly dressed in lies

The fact I feel no matter what I will
always care about him proves to me
I do not care about myself.

-or else I wouldn't

The butterflies that used to fly to every corner of my stomach for you are now replaced with rocks, sadness and Everclear. Forgive me while I forget you.

-gone

Every time he says he loves you after he hurts you, little devils dance through your mind and convince you it was your fault.

-wrong

my father warned me boys only want
you temporarily
like a number on a check.
to have his love you must tend to his
wants.
your boundaries open wider than your
legs before him,
there's no going back.
have you never learned to not build a
home around people?
Inescapable, his lips milk phrases of love
but
his reclusive aversion to "I love you" slips
your mind
in the way his fingers slip behind your
body
like a desperate fish on the line he has
you hooked.

-disgustingly good

The war inside my head is silent. My mouth is still. My heart is solemn. My thoughts are numb. My tears are the only thing that move.

-nothing left

I fell in love with his demons. Not because I thought they were angels, but because I had demons too.

-painfully similar

I shared a bed with you, but we never shared a home. So, I built one around you, but you opened the door I left unlocked one night after I confessed my love for you, and you left.

-homeless

I tried to guide his hands along my body
for where I feel the most, but he never
seemed to touch my heart.

-where have they been

I tried to breathe life into our love, but it was all a rouse. It never had a heartbeat.

-useless

Let another's love give you power, but
don't give them power over you, when they
do not love you.

-what my mother told me

My tears came to visit me again last
night. It's because of them I am
not alone.

- but I am

I wrote this book as my insides collapsed
and the only way out of this hell was to
write.

-echo

soft memories melt into the shape of a
bottle she pounds
when he forgets why he loved her
but remembers why he left.

-stop & go

When he beckons your name at midnight
you find yourself at hell's gate.
He bends you over so you can hear
echoes of a pieced together and drowned
out "I love you" just to keep the devil close.
Piece by piece, the hill becomes a mountain
and the puddle turns into an ocean as your
insecurities you named "him" undress your
broken heart. She wanted nothing more
than to be loved and, in his eyes, she saw
pain, and, in that pain, she saw herself.

-he is what you see in him

the pain

why do people assume sad poems are
written at night?
because hearts cry at all hours.
emptiness has no curfew.

-midnight

you see it was because I loved him so much, I trembled at the thought of losing him, but I of all people knew it would come. he would ride on gallantly through the night, swooping up girls like champagne spitting out of a bottle, unloosen the top and watch the rest tumble out. what must I do? my soul cries for hands I cannot hold and for a heart I must not love. but I do. I am but one in the night, he is no more mine than the moon is to people as it appears only after sunset and its beauty kisses us all... as all we see is the moon, and all it sees is us.

-fighting a losing battle

All your emptiness is full of sad stories
your soul cannot carry.

-heavy

Abuse is not always black eyes, scars and bruises, sometimes its climbing into bed with someone and feeling desperately alone.

-solitude

I have been sad before, don't get me
wrong.
But this time it was a little different.
Everything was gone. I was alone.
Hair pushed back over a toilet seat as my
pain crept up my throat and through my
mouth and told me how sad I really was.

-can't hide

The most difficult thing about discovering he lied and cheated, is to believe it. To imagine it. All of those nobody's became somebody to your somebody, and all of a sudden, you were nobody to your somebody and now your somebody is nobody. That shit hurts the most.

-10

your lips smelled like drugs
your tongue tasted like liquor
now I still can't see straight
and I've been high ever since

-height

If he wanted you to be the one, he would've treated you like the one. Don't lie to yourself.
He has lied enough already.

-familiar

The thing about loneliness is we will let anyone into our broken homes. We lock ourselves in and box the world out, hopelessly convinced one day someone will eventually come along. Our brokenness peeks through the side window, searching for anyone close enough to let in. This is how loneliness lives.

-knock

knock

You describe your pain in a foreign language I cannot understand. Point to where it hurts.

-heart

Poetry is all about what happens on the inside. Pain and emotions boil within us before bursting out in the form of words. So, I guess he was right, your tears mean nothing.

-deeper meanings

heart in hand I trudged perpetually into
the darkness
as I recognized it as my own.

-alone

You unequivocally learned sadness ran in your family when your father loved the bottle more than you and your mother remembered the names of her pills before your own name. Depression knocked on your door.
You were eleven.

-8 years ago

Read the invisible signs. Listen to them.
They're screaming at you.

-leave him!!!!

Love is not painful. If he rips your heart out and leaves you stumbling on the side of the road, do not dress him up as love.

-costumes and masks

The breaking became the hurting as the hurting became the healing. Do not keep him around. Even if he signs your casts in hearts and sweet words, he was the one who broke you. Every. Single. Time.

-patterns

Her life was like a picture. Worth a thousand words, with another thousand tears behind it.

-maybe more

Accept the pain he caused you
but use it to build. You will be stronger
for the next.
But more importantly, yourself.

-who to love first

The greatest gift you gave me was how to blindly love. To see every red flag and say *to hell with red- I rather paint hearts all over them.*
And suffer later.

-inevitable

it scared me truly
to imagine a seemingly eternal love
cut short by swords of lies and words
sliced deeper than any knife in my back
blood poured out like vodka in a shot
"I love you" meant nothing which is
exactly what he did

-empty

you wrote me love notes
but through the crackling of the paper
and the slits between the cursive
I always read

"I will leave you"
every single time.

-continue

and so, he stood there. arms folded across his chest with an arrogant look as if he had no idea how much he hurt me. as if we hadn't spent our high school years together whether in the front of a classroom or the back of a car or in the middle of this place we call life. my words hung dry in the air, as if I expected him to take my pain and bury them deep within himself. as if that would be enough to change him. the pieces of my broken heart lay across his feet, but he did not stumble. his firm jaw of which I used to kiss bore firm into his face, as if I expected him to mirror the troublesome part within him. every piece of him I knew. except for that. as if I thought I knew the darkness or would ever believe I would be able to tame it. I poured my soul into his heart, as if I thought he loved me. I dove deep into my tears without knowing how to swim, as if I believed he would save me.

-drown

I am deaf to echoes of a pieced together
and drowned out "I love you". I tried to
keep the devil close. He watched women
cascade along and manipulated his dirty
little fingers to puppet their every move.
I wanted to feel love, not burn because
of it.

-puppet master

I left a key under the mat by the front
door of my heart,
I always kept it locked, just to be safe.
Deadbolted, actually.
You said you loved me.
My doorbell would pierce the thin air
when pressed,
I was always aware of visitors.
I let no one in.
The windows were always shut, the
wooden panes rotted, and the glass stained
black.
You promised you loved me.
Everything was untouched.
Not a sound rippled through time.
But here you were, inside.
You didn't need the secret key.
You lied your way in.

-you never loved me

9am- (...)
11am- (...)
1pm- (...)
4pm-(...)
7pm- (...)

11:53pm- You up?
12:05am- Wyd?
12:28am- Come over.

-he only needs you at night

Let it hurt and hurt
And hurt
And hurt
It's part of the
Healing.

-never 100

if lies are all you have to feed me
please leave.
I'll take the check.
because I'd rather starve to death
than feed on your poison.

-killed me once

the wonder

Why do we tremble at the idea of being
left?
The concept of "not being enough"
Is frightening to me.
As if love justifies being strapped onto
another's soul, hoping they won't open the
door to their heart to let others in. As if we
should cling on with every piece of our
being in order to hold onto something that
will always find a way to escape. You cannot
cage the wind. It is free. It has no legs, no
being, no intentions of staying in one place
so why do we think anyone is more
powerful? If you fear being "left" what are
you holding onto?

-empty hands full of love

She looked at me and asked
Why do we hurt the ones who love us
No one really knows why. Humans just
seem to do that.
It's like
We believe the only way to face the
storm is to break down the walls that
surround us
That protect us
As if the person who gave you their
world was so much worse
Then the one who didn't

-where lies the truth

Whenever my father raises his voice
I see my mother quiver
I think
What is she thinking of
What has happened
To my poor mother
What does she show me
But not tell me
She proves to me she is strong
But I can see
She was not always
strong
I wonder how heavy her sorrow be-
What other names does Satan have?

-who was he

I watched as your eyes and fingers
carefully wrapped around her body like a
canvas
as you painted different colors
and I couldn't help but think you had
never handled me with such care
I was a rough draft as you found your
final copy in her soul
what had she done to deserve you

-ungodly

I want to sleep now
not because I really care
but because then you can't feel any pain
or miss anyone you shouldn't
while you sleep.
so I think it's magnificent
and I believe that's the real reason why
they say
"sleep is a beautiful thing"

-pray my soul to keep

I never believed in happy endings
because if it was all so great
why did it leave and cease to exist?
So where is the beauty in death and
loss?
I see no light in the inevitable.

-alas it came

My tears rolled down in hot pursuit, as if
they were desperately trying to find a place
on my body you had not been. You are no
longer
everywhere.

-where are you now

I always used to say
what
would
I
do
without
you
but soon enough I realized you can't ask
yourself questions
that one day you'll
find yourself answering.

-are you still there

Words dripped out of your mouth
like sandpaper on a stone
what a cruel
sound it makes.

-sticks and stones

Why do we forget dreams but remember
nightmares?
This question plagued my mind for a
while.
It's as if we need to remember the
sadness
or the fear
or the hatred.
Maybe this is why so many people find
darkness in their hearts.
They wish to live on because their fear is
to be forgotten.

-c'est la vie

light and dark cannot mix together at
once.
yet here you are.

-how

the jagged lines
of this poem
are so   uneven.
I tried to mirror it to
my
broken
heartstrings
that had

been

cut in a hurry.

-what do I listen to

If she is everything you've dreamed of,
why is it you keep dreaming?

-sheep

They say distance makes the heart grow
fonder,
But does that mean the farther you are, the
more you are loved?
Closeness of the hearts unwittingly sow the
seeds of apathy.
Is that why you disappeared?

-closeness of distance

I long so desperately to live in his arms and
heart forever
but my lease is almost up.

-evicted

They say, "how you get them is how you lose them." How he comes into your life is how he will exit. Not through a peephole, dark tunnel, or back door but through the exact same door. If pain and lies are his mother tongue, there isn't a damned thing you could do or say to make him unlearn the words his father taught him. I don't believe people can't change. I believe people won't change. He must change within himself because he deems it necessary. Worthy. You cannot convince him he must learn a new language if his father set him at his height and regurgitated every single phrase he has ever come to know. When his mother mirrors your bruises (also those on your heart), he will not change. He controls his tongue and his hands, and you cannot rewire this. The abuse you experience from the start will continue. You are not enough to change him; he must want it on his own. Begin with him when he is new. Begin when you speak the same language. Because if you don't, as

he is- will prove why you lost him. Why you
never truly had him.

-felt so real

You're searching for answers, aren't you? They say time heals all wounds, but in reality, it slaps an old band-aid on your heart and demands for you to accept his absence. As if he never really mattered. As if he was never really there. No longer.

-hourglass

You put a happy sign above your head and a smiling mask upon your face. You repeat, "I am fine" like a mindless parrot. You burden no one but yourself with your depression. No one must know you are hurting in places no one should feel such hurt. You seek the goodness in others especially when they don't deserve it. You subconsciously seek acceptance and result to loving their harmful flaws, in order to encourage a chance for yours to be loved as well. You tell yourself lesser is okay because you are lesser and small pieces can still make a whole. Together. Eventually. You think.

How is that going?

-you call that love?

Do animals fall out of love? Bald eagles, gray wolves, and swans mate for life. Do they not wake up and decide the other is not enough? Why don't they lie or cheat? How do their daily routes not encompass the search for something of which is not their own? How do they stay together through unwavering faith, trust, and love? On what prism or blueprint of life did this fail to cross over to humans?

-put to flight

My tears wouldn't let me sleep last night. They told me my heart was broken and asked me to write in order to numb the pain. I told them to leave so I could see clearly, but as soon I began to let my heart flow through the pen, they came right back again.

-out of ink   again

the epiphanies

unconditional love is under the condition
you stay.

-how fast can you run

humans are creatures of habit
which explains why you forgive him
every single time

-repeat

And so, I began bleeding and grieving
thinking it was just part of the process;
he shatters your heart, only to leave you
with one half of yourself broken
and the other half slipping through a
doorway
with blood on his hands and your scent
on his neck
is this not how we end?

-gone before you came

They say if you really love someone you
should let them go.
So you did,
but maybe he let go first.
Not because he loved you,
but because he didn't.

-how I learned

Love suppresses the pain of heartbreak,
which was caused by love.

-which comes first

and at that very moment something
inside me clicked
as I realized how silly life truly was
how you wrapped up all of life's
moments in your hand
and kept it close to your heart
with all of your yesterday's
all of your today's
and a seemingly endless amount of
tomorrow's
until one day you grow old and tired and
your hand loosens
and the memories fall out
and all of a sudden
"tomorrow"
becomes a day ceased to exist
and this is called life
and they say life is beautiful

-such is life

your eyes,
they were beautiful
and people say your eyes are the
windows to your soul
but yours were mirrors
your poor tired soul constantly changed
and masqueraded into things you were not
because of who you were surrounded by
then one day I didn't like the way I
looked when I gazed into them
and I shattered them
for my own egoistical pleasure
but only then did I realize that inside you
were lifeless and empty
so then the mirrors were gone and so
were you.

-reflection or real

And so, I'm left to remember the way his
eyes crinkled up
whenever he laughed
and how he would grab my waist before
kissing me
but now the tears run down to my lips
and
my god they're starting to forget.

-all the ways I miss you

Your presence surrounded me like
whiskey in a bottle
too much and I become drunk on the
feeling you're the one
too little and I become sober on the idea
you don't love me
but nowadays what's the difference?

-drunk on the idea of being sober

I wanted so desperately to mouth the
words I love you to her.
To fill a seemingly unfillable void of
reclusion
To stop denying my affection for true
beauty
lighting the world on fire with my
passion for her eternal soul
I was stuck in my own labyrinth and the
only way out was to admit it, but
My words would be a simple ripple in
time
Only to be lost in senseless urgency
Undiscovered in depths of mindless
space
An utter gleam of intention below the
surface
But I remained quiet as my powerless
eyes danced
between her movements
through the door.
I was stuck inside but she remained free.
Sometimes love isn't about obtaining but
appreciating
She was beautiful, wild and courageous

so, I shut my lips and let her vanish
before me
but I could never let her go.

-she was the one

and in that very moment I felt everything
and nothing all at once
sadness, regret, nostalgia, anger, pain,
but yet I was empty
I was a cup
and his sweet words were water
he filled me up completely
until he realized he wasn't thirsty
and emptied me down a drain
and in that moment, I was forever
destined to be eternally scared of promises
because they're like glass in a mirror
they become what you perceive them to
be
and when it breaks it hurts
as the pieces cling into your skin and
pierce your soul
it opens you up and empties you
completely.
a rush of emotion fills your tired heart
it can't take it anymore
you can't take it anymore
so, you let go
and as the emotions scream inside you

they finally burst out of your lifeless
body
and so, in that very moment you feel
nothing and everything all at once.

-parched

You never truly know what abuse is.
Even when it slaps you across the face
then kisses your wounds.
The devil is
human too.

-red

you loved sweet tea
he loved sweet tea
but although his eyes betrayed him
it was clear he no longer loved you.
so, you poured the sweet tea down the
drain
as your soul indents towards the sun
moving through oblivion
and so, you will drink unsweetened tea
because the color of it resembles the
color of his eyes
that spoke volumes of love but disguised
itself to corrupt beautiful lies
and so, small tears will form on your cup
as they cascade down your face
the bitter aftertaste transpires into your
soul
but whatever would you do without it?
the darkness and bitterness embodied
your past with him
so, you will rather hold onto the deepest
black of his soul

then be rid of him echoing your memory
and so, you will drink unsweetened tea.
-bittersweet

so, I strung along with an open-ended
wound in my heart
as the band aid dangled from my soul
I was a hellish mess
so how is it you look at me like that
with those beautiful blue eyes
I could fall for them.
you called me stunning that night
as I shook and fumbled my fingers into
the same kind of knot I felt in my throat
I lost my balance for a moment, but your
eyes remained locked,
I apologized for my clumsiness.
I was clearly confused as my mind raced
into a maze
but the only way out of the labyrinth
was the answer of why you looked at me
like that
no one has ever really looked at me the
way you do.

-have you seen yourself

and so, I spent my nights scribbling down ideas
as to why you stopped loving me.
I connected the dots with thin lines on
every single word of explanation
and witnessed an incredible form of art,
but it's meaning I would never understand
until I realized this was my answer.

-unclear

they told me to drink
until you came back but when would this
be?
keep pouring the bottles and counting
the shots
until all I can do is mutter your name.
don't stop the flow of alcohol until I
finally forget why you left,
my head pounded inside me
as I barely managed to crack my eyes
open an inch
and suddenly I saw you standing before
me
and that's when I knew I had drank
enough.

-17..18...

I thanked God every day for your
presence
not physically with me
but for giving up one of his angels
to live on earth.
I never told you this,
but it doesn't matter
because I stopped.
we stopped.
and left the past as it was
so, I always used to thank God every day
for your presence
until you were no longer present.

-moderation

eternal is not real
neither are you

neither were we.

-how about now

you are the sum and the difference of all
your lonely tears and sleepless nights.
if he really loved you, they wouldn't have
been lonely or even there at all. your tear
ridden cheeks would be bare as would your
body, because if he was there that's all he
really truly wanted.
he didn't love you. he loved the idea of
you. the feel of you. the spontaneous mix of
emotions that settled into his body because
of you.
a simple pleasure made simpler by
saying "I love you" and watching you tense
up and comply,
but he fell asleep in bed. because he was
tired. not of you. but of having you.
you were more than what he could ever
deserve
because he was weak, and you were
strong.
so he couldn't run fast enough to keep
up with you, so he slept, and you cried
as he trailed behind, only to be lost in
the shadows

and never seen again by your hollowed
eyes
the gut-wrenching feeling of pain never
left your soul that night. you will forever
continue trying to fill the emptiness
for the rest of your existence without
him.
but this will happen every day
and they call this the evolution of love
even though it never seems to evolve.

-love ?

writing is just like
endlessly scouring the dark
for all the reasons why
you're up so late
and why your heart can't stop bleeding
words
and why a piece of a paper is your band
aid
and why there's no one else around,
but you.

-I know

The irony behind everyone pretending is
it becomes our reality.

-home

I see the cuts on my body in all the
places I slowly chipped away in order to try
and become your idea of perfect. But
through trying to be closer to you, I drifted
farther
and
farther
away
from myself.

-so far gone

your absence reminded me of that book
I never read.
you told me you loved its story
because it reminded you of us
but one day you hurdled it into the
street
and that night it poured.
The seams broke
the pages tore and
it mirrored my soul.
as deep gasps tore from my heart
the book was gone
and so were you.

-chapter 2

Black
White
Cold
Hot
Hate
Love
You
Me
One fails to exist without its opposite
I existed for you
You existed without me.

-yes.

no.

the stars align above and tell me to leave
you, but sadly I am always looking down
because that is how you look at me.

-tiny

the hope

my eyes were heavy as my eyelids
fluttered
my head nodded to sleep but small
jitters kept me from shutting them.
my hands trembled as my mind searched
for darkness;
I was so incredibly tired,
but you were right in front of me.
and I guess you cared less or were even
more tired or my presence didn't affect you
because exhaustion overcame
as your eyes gave in to rest
your lips slowly parted but no words
escaped
nevertheless,
despite all the beautiful dreams I had
about you
and the happiness it filled my soul
I couldn't find myself to shut my eyes
because at that moment
nothing was more magnificent than
watching you sleep.

-only the sweetest of dreams

Tell me you hate me
Instead of
You love me
So I'm okay with never seeing you again.

-at peace

Ruins shatter before they break.
But I am not ruined.

-he ~~tried~~ failed

you are still whole
without his half.

-avoid

My heavy heart weighed me down like a smooth stone against the current.
I will either sleep well tonight or not at all.

-sleepless love

she was a living embodiment of hope
and dreams
she tasted of warmth and champagne
let me have a sip
before you leave

-already gone

if I told you
why I left
would you still
let
me
go?

-the good in goodbye

that man could say he loves you
but don't confuse
love with hate.

both are very passionate.
but one will kill you slowly
and the other
even slower.

-which is which

and then one day I couldn't stop writing
your eyes reminded me of verses
your soul was a rhyme
and your smile brought similes
and so, I wrote until my fingers bled
and blood hit the page
and only then I realized that from now
on you were
every small slice of poetry
I would ever come to write.

-ABAB

my emotions run dry like the words in
my mouth
explaining what you mean to me.

-desert

5 months. You waited 5 months. To call.
To check up. As if there would be any less
casualties by waiting. That long. You make
sure. I am okay. When I left your
apartment. With tears running just as fast.
You let me go. Leave just like that. So, you
call. To check up. To make sure. I know. You
have power. Over me. But I pick up. 5
months later. As if. You know. I know.
I will hang up.

-try

My grandma walked down from heaven and gave my mother a hug. She told her that she missed her and that her love did not die with her. I didn't see it, but I didn't need my eyes to feel it. It was the moment she touched her tombstone and caressed her name. My middle name. I've never met my grandma, but I thank her for my mother. I hate to see her cry.

-Clary

Love is just like endlessly scouring the dark for all the reasons why our hearts flutter at a mere glimpse or why their presence makes the darkness so much brighter. Love forces us to surrender yet it conquers all battles. For all the days you've brought me light, I've loved you even more.

-lost and finally found

Life moves on even when you don't.

-go to sleep

The strongest form of revenge is to remove all power it has over you. What good is the devil if hell doesn't exist.

-strip all power

Take your flowers and broken heartstrings and unroot them from his garden of weeds. Never let him walk all over you again. He will rip your petals and tear up your stems, not even your thorns can stop him.
Leave.

-escape artist

If he is all you see, close your eyes.
If he is all you hear, do not listen.
If he is all you want to touch, hold
yourself tight.
Ignore everything about him.
Recognize your heartbeat.
You do not need him.

-scissors

The fact that he isn't thinking about you anymore is the most comforting yet painful feeling in the world.

-glue

Like a sheep in wolves' skin,
You create a façade of strength on the
outside, but within you are weak.
I can see your wool.

-shorn

I stood there
with my arms crossed over my chest
as if my frail arms were strong enough to
keep out your soul
and protect my battered heart
you quickly learned to seep through my
hands
and interweave my fingers
to pry open my weakness
and touch my broken pieces

-open wider

How he left
told the story of why
he came.

- all for nothing

I scratched out the note he had left for me. As if I were to sit here and believe he loved me. After all, he was magnificent and all the girls adored him, while I was the genetic makeup of 2 parts inadequate and 3 parts insecure. He spent his time describing why he loved me, but I would roll my eyes without knowing how far back they were capable of going. I would test his devotion to me, by occasionally wearing something tight or letting my hair loose, but he always looked at me as if I had just aligned every single star known to mankind with my bare hands in the backyard of his childhood home. Strange, I thought. Boys typically knew easier was better, and I considered myself rather puzzling. I preferred leading a prospect on before dropping him and inducing a familiar central pain, instead of having my body clawed in the backseat of a Jeep explorer in a parking lot of a venue on a list of places "a young girl should not go."

It worked out for me because I rather be wanted than loved, but this time I felt both.

-you are everything to me

The echoes of "I love you" fell deaf as I rather be chased then tied up. I lust the fear of love. It will never find me.

-there I was

I have found some things in life to be
meaningless until you give them power.

-you are so powerful

Made in the USA
Columbia, SC
18 February 2020